WANT TO CLAIM ALL THE RESOURCES DISCUSSED IN THE BOOK?

HEAD ON OVER TO ETHICALLYPROFIT.COM/BOOK AND GRAB THEM BEFORE YOU DIG IN!

RF

TABLE OF CONTENTS

RF

RF

ABOUT THE AUTHOR

Roland is a "recovering attorney" and co-founder/principal of 5 different Inc. Magazine fastest growing companies in the e-commerce, e-learning, real estate and SaaS spaces.

He is a serial entrepreneur who has founded, scaled or sold over two dozen different businesses ranging from consumer products to live events to manufacturing companies with sales ranging from $3 million to just under $4 billion.

Currently CEO of All Channels Media, LLC, and principal in Scalable. co, DigitalMarketer.com, Traffic & Conversion Summit, Praxio.com, TruConversion.com, War Room Mastermind, Fully Accountable, Everbowl Restaurants, Big Block Realty, Scribe Publishing and Real Estate Worldwide.

Roland has been featured in Entrepreneur, Forbes, Money, Business Insider, Fast Company and on major television networks. And he has interviewed Sir Richard Branson, Spanx founder Sarah Blakely and many other industry leaders on his award winning Business Lunch podcast.

Roland's work includes infomercials with Guthy-Renker, publishing deals with Simon & Schuster and Random House, shows with major hotels on the Las Vegas strip, over 100 private and public offerings, running an international hedge fund, advising major brands on a variety of business and legal related issues (from PepsiCo to MacDonald's).

Roland has a real passion for business and putting deals together and is always looking for businesses to invest in or acquire, re-position and sell. Recent strategic partnerships and clients include Microsoft, Southwest Airlines, Etihad Airlines, Harper-Collins Publishing, Fedex and Uber.

His specialities include acquiring or partnering with entrepreneurs to scale businesses through acquisitions, strategic relationships and marketing. Roland is also adept at negotiation, copywriting, marketing strategy, structuring and funding of mergers and acquisitions and, public exit strategies for businesses and entrepreneurs.

INTRODUCTION
EPIC PROFITS IN CRISIS

When COVID-19 signaled a potential recession, some business owners were fearful. They worried their hard work would evaporate into thin air and they'd lose everything. While recessions are certainly a challenging time, I saw an opportunity to make epic profits by helping business owners in need of selling their business (we'll discuss how to do that shortly).

As the price of buying a business dropped because buyers disappeared and nervous sellers scrambled to sell, I started to buy. I also began to teach others how to see the same opportunity with my Ethical Profits in Crisis (E.P.I.C) Accelerator.

This isn't something that's happened once or twice. You can see a steady pattern in the graph below that shows when a recession occurred and what happened to deal multiples afterward.

Deal multiples have generally increased

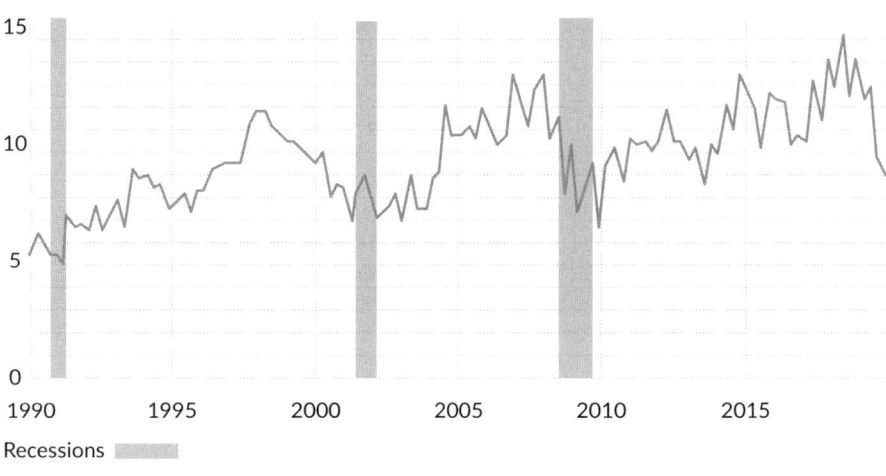

Recessions ▓▓▓▓▓

Source: PwC analysis of Refinitiv data, National Bureau of Economic Research

---

Deal multiples are how businesses are valued. If the multiple goes down, you can buy the company for less. If a multiple goes up, you can sell it for more. To figure out the multiple of a business, divide the asking price by the cash flow.

As vaccines roll out and state officials begin to reopen their cities, we know now more than ever that business values are going to rise again *and soon.*

This is the opportunity that we have right now.

We can still buy businesses for low prices and make epic profits quickly—if you're willing to learn what it takes to make deals like this happen.

RF

CHAPTER 1

BECOMING AN EPIC INVESTOR

Between 2019 and 2020, I owned, built, and sold 24+ businesses with sales from $3M-$3B+. I had 3 exits and 3 acquisitions, but that's not even the point of this book. You can find plenty of books on growing and acquiring businesses.

What you can't find are books telling you how to do it with a $0 investment.

It's important to start to wrap your mind around this concept as early into this book as possible. This is something that is happening all around you—in every niche. Even if you think your industry is too niche for this type of deal, I'm here to let you know...it's not.

This is a list of *some* of the industries I've acquired businesses in that have gone on to sell for less than $10 million to even $1 billion.

<$10M
- Trade Shows/Events
- Digital Marketing Agency
- Legal Services

- Corporate Training
- Document Preparation
- Tax Services

$10M

- eLearning
- Commercial Real Estate
- Motorcycle Equipment
- Direct Response
- Mastermind Groups
- Supplements
- Real Estate Training
- Online Casinos
- eCommerce
- Medical Equipment
- Telecom Infrastructure
- Beauty + Cosmetics
- Software as a Service

$100M

- Medical Billing
- Machine Manufacturing
- CPG

$1B+

- Residential Real Estate

Because of this list, I can confidently say *I'm sure this will work for you.*

How did these business opportunities happen for me? Looking back, I can see 5 E.P.I.C opportunities that I was able to use to a build resume like this:

In 1981-1982, I acquired a manufacturing company using a process called Leverage Buy-Out.

In 1990-1991, I got introduced to the retail industry and acquired a company using a workouts strategy.

In 2000-2001, the Dotcom bubble gave me the opportunity to reorganize companies.

In 2007-2009, I started to invest in real estate companies through roll-ups.

Today, I'm investing primarily in publishing and MRR companies with $0 out-of-pocket investments—without ever taking advantage of a single person.

THE 3 CRISES MOTIVATING PEOPLE TO SELL THEIR BUSINESS (RIGHT NOW!)

We don't take advantage of business owners, because it's just not good karma. It's not who we are or what we practice, and that's not what you're going to learn in this book. We're looking to actually be helpful, with the goal of finding an opportunity to profit while also helping someone else out.

There are 3 crises that are motivating people to sell their businesses right now.

The first of crisis comes from the baby boomers. They're aging out and want to transition their businesses. There are 50 million baby boomers that want to retire over the next 10 years. All of these people, who are trying to move on to the next phase of their lives, can't retire until there's something that happens with their businesses. Here's where there is a really giant opportunity for us to the tune of four and a half million businesses a year.

The second crisis is a market inefficiency and overcapacity in the smaller business space. To be clear, these small businesses aren't the Mom and Pop shops down the road from your house making $100,000 a year. I'm talking about small businesses as defined by investment bankers—businesses making $10 million or less. For these companies, there isn't a set place they can exit through a sale to the public (like larger companies can through an IPO). That doesn't mean they *don't want to sell*, it just means their chances of getting the option are smaller.

The third crisis comes from business failures. With 6 million startups established every year, 1.6 million of them are going to fail. Investors, like you and I, can buy these companies and avoid all of the risks that come with a start up. We can bypass the high failure rate of starting a business from scratch and buy one that's already made it out of that danger zone. Even venture capitalists in Silicon Valley fail 75% of the time—with E.P.I.C you can avoid becoming one of those statistics.

MERGERS AND ACQUISITIONS FOR GROWTH

Why does buying businesses make sense compared to the other things you can do with your time and money?

Investing in businesses to buy and sell, can give you on average a 44% return. This outperforms putting money into a savings account by 4,037%, investing in the S&P by 550%, and even buying real estate investments by 415%.

ROI by Investment Category

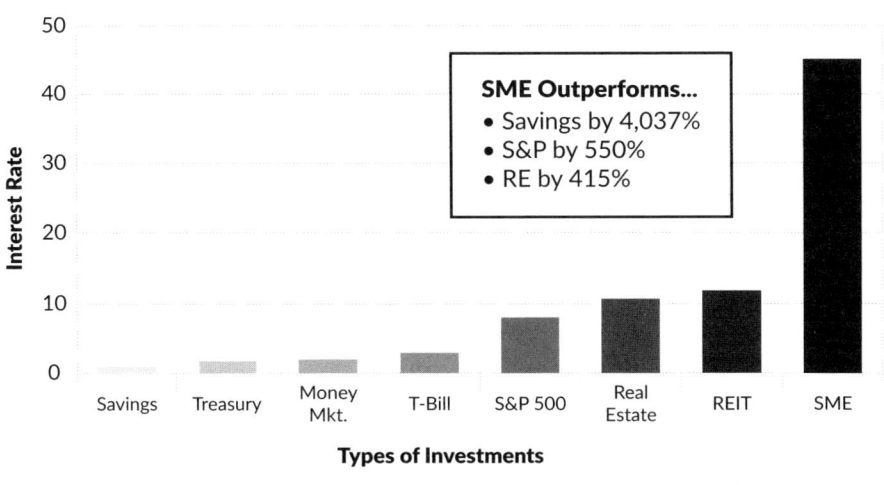

Now, let's compare the returns between buying a business and starting your own. Have you ever felt more inclined to start your own business and build it from the ground up?

While that may feel like the less risky option—it's actually the complete opposite.

When you buy a business instead of starting your own, you get these benefits:

1. Less risk
2. More financing options
3. Established brand recognition
4. Instant customers
5. Instant sales

6. Instant profits
7. Instant contacts (leads, suppliers, etc.)
8. Instant employees

And, you'll get to step out of the 90% startup failure statistics (even 75% of VC deals fail!).

Even acquiring costs less than a start up. When you compare the amount of cash invested, available funding, valuation, profit margins, and EBITDA/SDE (Earnings Before Interest, Taxes, Depreciation and Amortization and Seller's Discretionary Earnings)—investing is the cheaper option.

Acquisition vs. Start-Up

	ACQUISITION	START-UP
Cash Invested	$50k	$50k
Leveraged Funding	$950k	$165k
Valuation	$1M++	$199k++
Profit Margin	10%**	10%**
EBITDA/SDE	$357k	$71k+
	2%	90%

This is where mindset comes in. As an investor, you need to make a mental shift called "The O-Myth".

You have to stop thinking about building your own business and working for that business or on that business. If you're opening the store, making coffee, serving customers, ordering supplies, and sweeping the floors—you work for your business. If you're hiring an operator, installing systems, creating processes, and building your community—you're working on your business.

This isn't what the really wealthy people are doing. These people are working above their business. They're finding investors, acquiring competitors, integrating supply and distribution chains, and acquiring new verticals.

Make The O-Myth mental shift as quickly as possible, so you stop working for or on your business and start working above it.

THE DEAL LIFECYCLE & ARBITRAGE OPPORTUNITIES

The Deal Lifecycle is the 18 steps of an investment deal, starting with finding opportunities to buy and ending with due diligence. You'll see the Deal Lifecycle below, the gray steps are the steps that we'll be covering in this book.

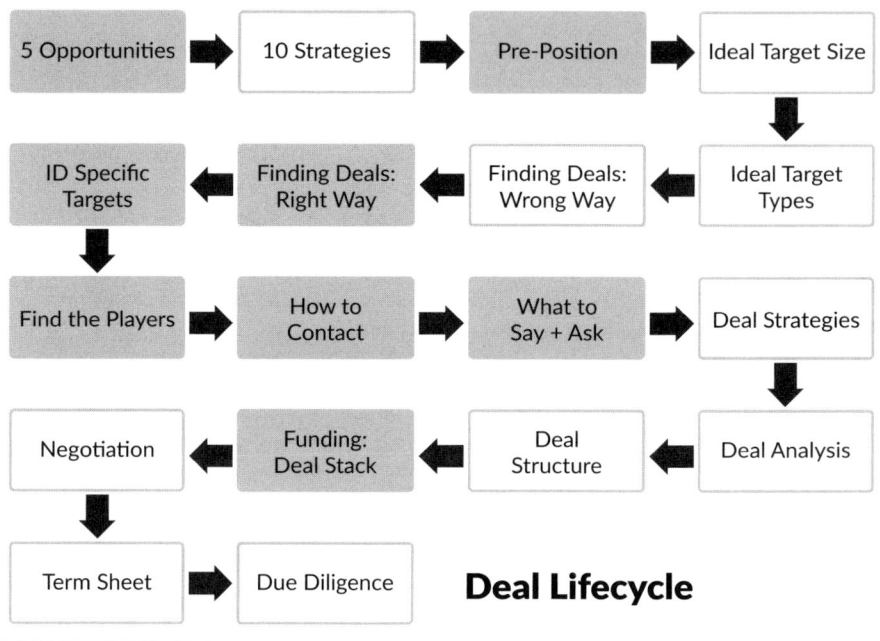

Deal Lifecycle

One of the very first steps of the Deal Lifecycle is to figure out what a business's value is. This tells you if you're willing to buy the business or not. Every investor has their own parameters for what they're looking for, and would consider a good deal.

For example, I want to buy companies that have a maximum 3.7x multiple, which correlates to the first two boxes below. I don't buy businesses in the fourth box because those are public companies, which tends to make things more complicated. What I will do is flip my 2.5x and 3.7x multiple companies into 12x and 24x multiples—and then sell them.

SME > PE > IPO Multiple Arbitrage

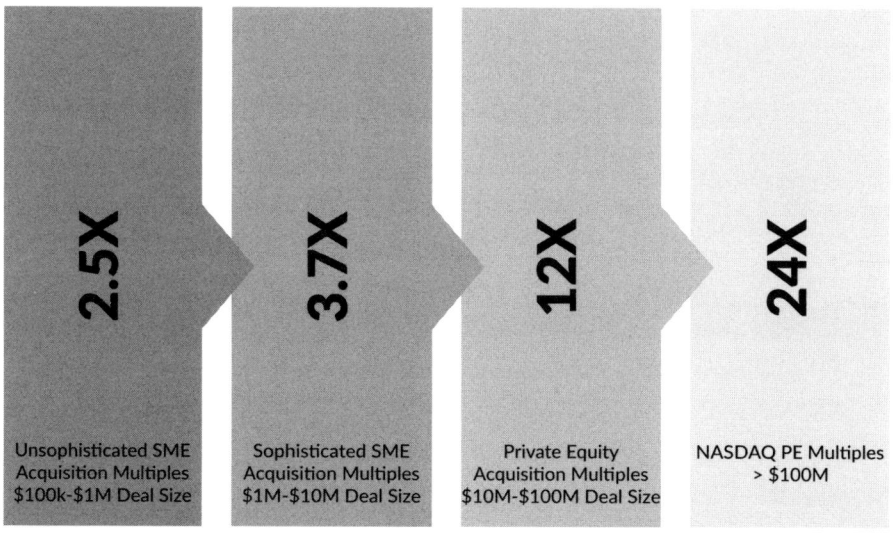

2.5X	3.7X	12X	24X
Unsophisticated SME Acquisition Multiples $100k-$1M Deal Size	Sophisticated SME Acquisition Multiples $1M-$10M Deal Size	Private Equity Acquisition Multiples $10M-$100M Deal Size	NASDAQ PE Multiples > $100M

These companies are generally closing and want to be sold, or are willing to give equity in return for me helping them in some way. These are arbitrage opportunities, which is just fancy investment jargon for buying low and selling high (I'll explain how I'm selling my equity below).

ARBITRAGE OPPORTUNITIES: CLOSINGS

Every year 595,000 businesses simply close and these businesses aren't all struggling to make ends meet. Some of them are doing incredibly well, but the owners are retiring and don't have any relatives or friends that want to run their business. Other business owners get overwhelmed by crises (like the current COVID-19 situation) or are just no longer passionate about their business and just want to get out.

That's a huge opportunity to buy.

Here are the top reasons businesses close:

1. Money
2. Retirement
3. Relocation
4. Burn-out
5. Health
6. Shiny object syndrome
7. Up-cycle (When the economy is up people think about selling)
8. Partner challenges
9. Death of the owner (As an owner operated business)

Here's what you'd be looking for from a business that's going to be closing to make sure that you're getting a good, better, or great deal.

Acquire Pre-Close @ Lower M

	GOOD	BETTER*	GREAT*
EBITDA of Target	$360k	$360k	$360k
Purchase Price Multiple	3.7x	1.5x	1x
Purchase Price	$1.3M	$540k	$360k
10% Cash out of Pocket	$130k	$54k	$36k
Valuation Post Closing	$1.3M	$1.3M	$1.3M

* Acquire @ under market multiple before the business closes   +$760k - $940k

And here's the ROI of buying a closing business, again as good, better, and great. By buying a business like this, you can see at the bottom that by Year One, you'll be making positive cash flow.

ROI: Buying A Closing Business

	GOOD	BETTER*	GREAT*
90% Loan Carry	$1.2M	$486k	$324k
10% Interest on Loan	($120k)	($48.6k)	(32.4k)
10% Cash out of Pocket	($130k)	($54k)	($36k)
	($250k)	($102.6k)	($68.4k)
Cash OOP+ Interest			

* Acquire @ under market multiple before the business closes

The return on your money...is insanely fantastic.

ARBITRAGE OPPORTUNITY: EQUITY DEALS

In these deals, instead of buying a company (like you bought the closing company above) you'd be offering your efforts in return for equity. This gives you a $0 dollar out of pocket investment and equity in a business.

This happens all the time. Let's say that you want to buy a rocket science company—you don't need to be a rocket scientist to help that company. All you have to do is figure out how to add value. This is called "earn-in to equity."

Here are 3 ways to earn-in equity:

1. You can be an advisor for 1% to 5% interest in the company
2. You can help them with growth for 10%-50% of the company (Growth Assist)
   a. This can be outright or under the terms that IF you can grow the company by X then you'll get YY%
3. You can help business owners exit their company and get 5% to 10% of the company in return (Exit Assist)

The key with earn-in to equity is not to take immediate equity. Instead, you want to take warrants, options, or phantom equity (this helps you avoid taxes).

When you get paid as an earn-in to equity investor, you'll get one of the below:

- A lump sum or monthly cash and any expenses
- Performance-based cash kicker
- Put option with predetermined value or easy exit
  - This gives you the option to exit when you're ready
- Call option with performance-based trigger
  - You'll earn an option to get equity in a company if you perform at a certain level

Now, you're going to need people to believe that you're the person to sell their business to or give equity options to. And that starts and ends by being the person that they're looking for.

HOW TO GET PEOPLE TO TALK TO YOU ABOUT SELLING THEIR COMPANY

What do all of these business owners have in common? They're all interested in money!

When you approach them as an investor, you are the thing that they were looking for. You just have to make sure they can recognize that.

Here's your first assignment of this book, it's time to make sure that you're positioned as an investor. On social media, you need to say that you're an investor so that your profiles showcase that...you're actually an investor. Take the time to make yourself known as an investor because when people know that you're an investor—they'll come to YOU with deals.

Take a look at how I've positioned my social media profiles to show that I'm an investor.

Position Yourself As Investor

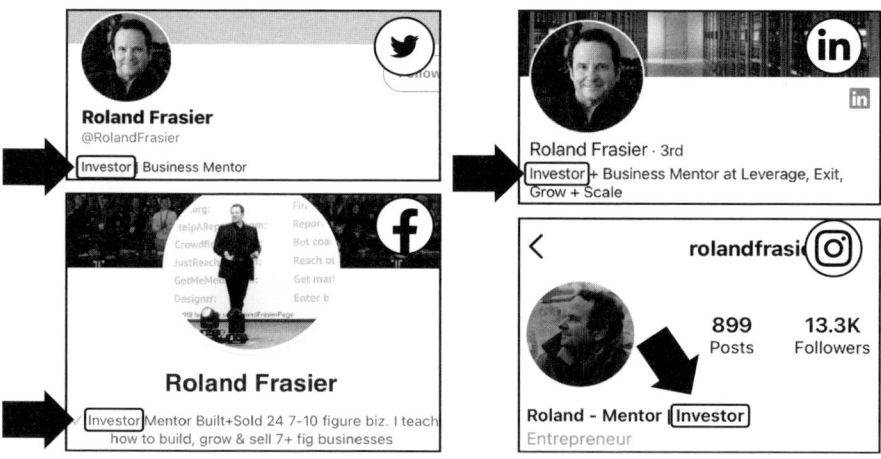

RF
ALWAYS USE AN SPV

The last thing you need to know about being an epic investor is the liability around investing. You don't want to be personally liable for the debts of the company. This is why you'll get a Special Purpose Vehicle.

> **"The one thing I know now that I wish I had known when I got started is the SPV. It would have saved me tens of millions of dollars."**
>
> *– Gary Vaynerchuk*

An SPV is a limited liability entity that you form to use for a deal, especially in an acquisition, spin-out, split-off, carve-out or joint venture. You use it to create a bright line that isolates liability from a proposed transaction in an entity from your personal or other business assets and income that you have.

My advice is to form an SPV immediately so that you always have one available for deals when they come up. You can use LegalZoom, BizFilings, or file for one yourself. If you don't have a lot of money, you can wait until you start a deal. The challenge with waiting is that it can take 2-3 weeks to get an SPV set up. Ideally, you want this ready as soon as it makes sense for you.

BEFORE YOU MOVE ON TO THE NEXT SECTION:

1. **Reposition Yourself as an Investor:** Add "investor" to your Linkedin and social media profiles, About Page, bio, and email signature
2. **Form an SPV:** Use a service like LegalZoom or BizFilings or file one yourself
3. **Review Arbitrage Opportunities.**

CHAPTER 2
HOW TO FIND BUSINESSES TO BUY

Starting to get excited? You're learning what you need to know to become an EPIC investor—and now it's time to get into your starting point. How do you even find businesses to buy? In this section, I'll show you where to find businesses to buy, the easiest types of businesses to buy, and how to buy traffic assets.

In the Deal Lifecycle, we're in the Ideal Target Types step.

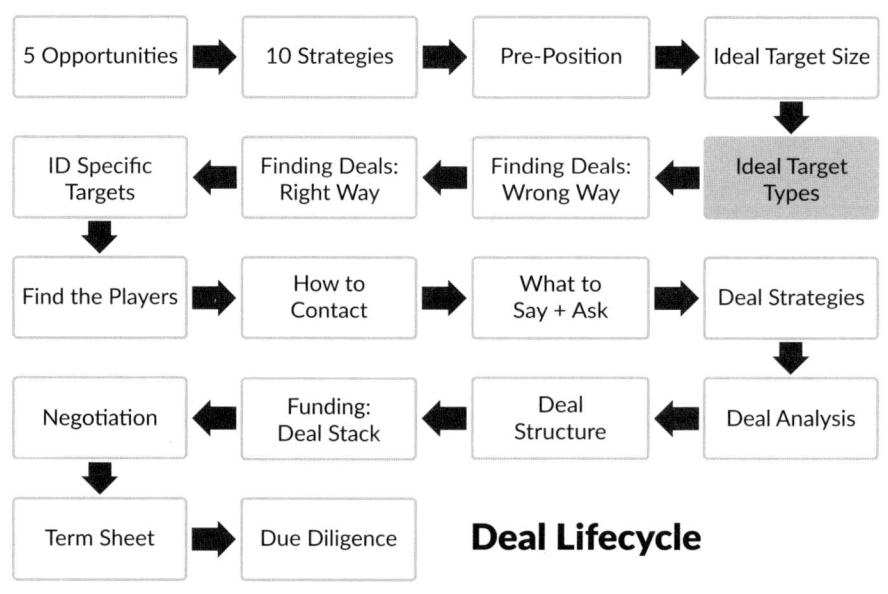

To start to find companies that make sense for you to buy, find a public company in your industry to use as a comparable company. What this means is that you're going to be looking for businesses they have acquired to get an idea of what they're buying—and what you should be buying.

To be clear, you're not trying to buy the companies that they're acquiring. But, if a comparable business to yours has just bought a CRM software company, that tells you that it might be beneficial for your company to buy a different CRM software company.

To find the businesses that a public company has acquired, Google "[COMPANY NAME]" + "Acquisitions"".

This will give you a list of the acquisitions the comparable company made. Make a list of these companies and see what might make sense for you.

A CASE STUDY IN FINDING BUSINESSES TO BUY

Let's say you own an accounting firm and you want to find businesses to buy that will help you grow that business.

Step #1: Google "publicly held + [category]"

First, Google "publicly held accounting firm" using the template [publicly held] + [category]. In this case, you have thirty-one million results. If you don't find a publicly held comparable company, then Google "[largest] + [category]", for example, "largest accounting firms".

For the search "publicly held accounting firm", the four biggest companies showed up as the first search result. They are Deloitte, Ernst & Young, KPMG, and PricewaterhouseCoopers.

Step #2: Identify Key Comparables

Once you find a company in your industry, Google, "[Company Name]" + "Acquisitions"—for example, "Deloitte Acquisitions". Review the list of the acquisitions this comparable company has made and note the types of companies it acquired (again, you can keep a spreadsheet to keep track). This gives you an idea of what was worth acquiring to these companies, and you can start to find the types of companies that would make sense for you to acquire.

Make a list of the types of companies the comparable company acquired that make sense for you.

For example, when we Googled "Deloitte Acquisitions", we found a website page from Deloitte dedicated to talking about their acquisitions and investments.

Deloitte.   Services ⌄   Industries ⌄   Insights ⌄   Careers ⌄

Strategic alignment

Each of our acquisitions must meet strict criteria for "strategic fit." Does an acquisition prospect complement and leverage our other services? Does it align with who we are and who we want to become? Does it enhance our culture and reflect our values? Does it adhere to our independence guidelines?

If you are an investment banker, venture capitalist, private equity investor, owner / entrepreneur or other individual representing a company that wants to be acquired, we'd like to hear from you. But first, get to know us a little by reviewing some key areas of our website. Understand our deep concern for ethics and independence, our commitment to inclusion, and our support for our communities.

Then, when we searched for Deloitte in Crunchbase, it showed the 39 acquisitions they just made. Not all companies are in Crunchbase which is why you want to look at huge companies during this stage. As you dive into this, you can find out what kind of companies these big companies in your industry are acquiring.

For example, Deloitte acquired an app and CRM business, a cloud service business, and a Salesforce integration business. These are adjacency acquisitions. When you're looking at expanding your business, you can ask, "What are all the things that I can sell to my client and does it make sense for me to acquire those companies so I can do cross referrals?". That's definitely what Deloitte is asking themselves.

You can also review the "Investments" tab on Crunchbase. Usually what precedes an acquisition is a small investment in what they want to acquire which gives you another hint as to what they're interested in.

Step #3: Keep researching each category of your business to find more comparable businesses

Step #4: Repeat the Google/Crunchbase search process for each comparable you identify to find acquisitions

Step #5: Make a list of the acquisitions for each major comparable business

Step #6: When you are done, you should have an extensive list of the ideal type of businesses to acquire to grow your business

Here's a pretty cool bonus—you didn't spend any money to get this information! While I definitely recommend a Crunchbase subscription, they offer a free trial period that you can take advantage of.

THE EASIEST TYPES OF BUSINESSES TO BUY IF YOU HAVE AN EXISTING BUSINESS

With an existing business, you have a lot of extensions of that business you may not realize are acquisition opportunities. For every business, there are 7 other types of businesses that can be acquired that would make sense to buy.

These businesses are:

Core Business Competitors: Make a list of your direct and indirect competitors for the business that you have or think you want to buy

Media: Make a list of the media that aggregates the eyeballs of your ideal client (This could be a company or a traffic asset)

Team and Resources: What would you like to have but don't want to develop them yourself?

Service Vendors: Vendors giving services to your customers

Product Vendors: Vendors giving your ideal customer products

Supply and Distribution: Supplying and distributing essentials to your ideal customers (For example, an ecommerce company that sells through affiliate businesses can buy that affiliate business)

Intellectual Property: Patents, pre-built information products, etc. that you can sell to your existing customers

Once you buy all of these companies and they start doing business with each other, this can easily become a 7x increase in your current business.

© 2019 Roland Frasier

For example, my company The Scalable Company bought:

Media: DIY Projects Facebook group with 250,000 members and we merged it with our DIY Ready Yourself Facebook Group (250,000 members), doubling our lead list for $1,500

Team + Resources: TruConversion was a vendor to us with a software team that we didn't have to build

Service Vendors: We were referring a lot of people out to Graphic Connections Group and we were able to acquire an interest in that company

Product Vendors: We have an online store for survival gear so we bought Banana Bay Tactical in Austin, Texas so we had the ability to get all of the dealerships that the brick-and-mortar store had and then sell those products in our online store

Supply + Distribution: We sell personal water filters for our company, and so we bought Coleman Filter Company

Intellectual Property: We bought Business Book Source for our start up company that provided business plans for Mom & Pop type businesses because they already had 128 plans and Excel spreadsheets

RF

If you're stuck on businesses to buy look at each of these 7 categories as even more. For example, media includes advertising, broadcasting, print publications, digital media, and production studios. Here are more ideas on companies you could buy:

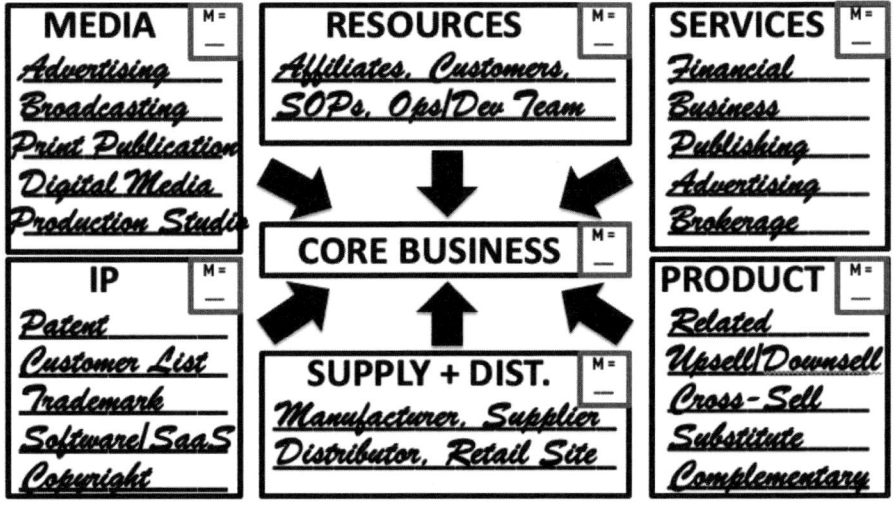

Fill out the Related Business Worksheet for your own business, adding in the multiple of what you can expect to pay for each business based on the industry (which I'll show you how to find in the last section of this book).

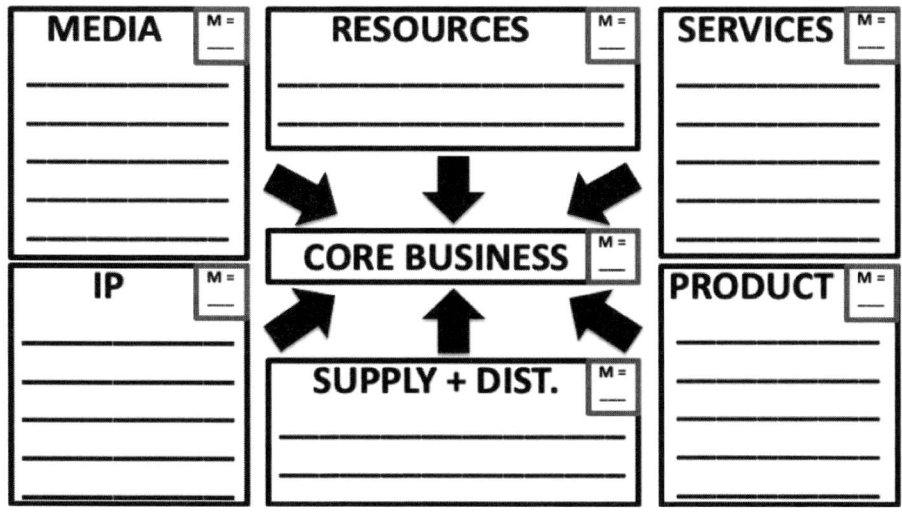

Start with the categories listed above and figure out what companies you can buy within that category, even the sub categories (for example, media → print publications). This will give you a huge list of strategic acquisitions.

TRAFFIC ASSETS OWN DON'T RENT: ZERO DOLLAR TRAFFIC

Do you advertise on Facebook, Google, LinkedIn, etc.?

What we don't typically think about is that we're renting—not owning—when we advertise on these platforms. In the real estate world, the people that make the most money don't rent... they own. In the online traffic world, it works the same way. We want you to own your traffic assets.

Here are the 7 traffic assets you can buy:

© 2019 Roland Frasier

And like on the previous page, you can break down each of these categories into subcategories, as seen below.

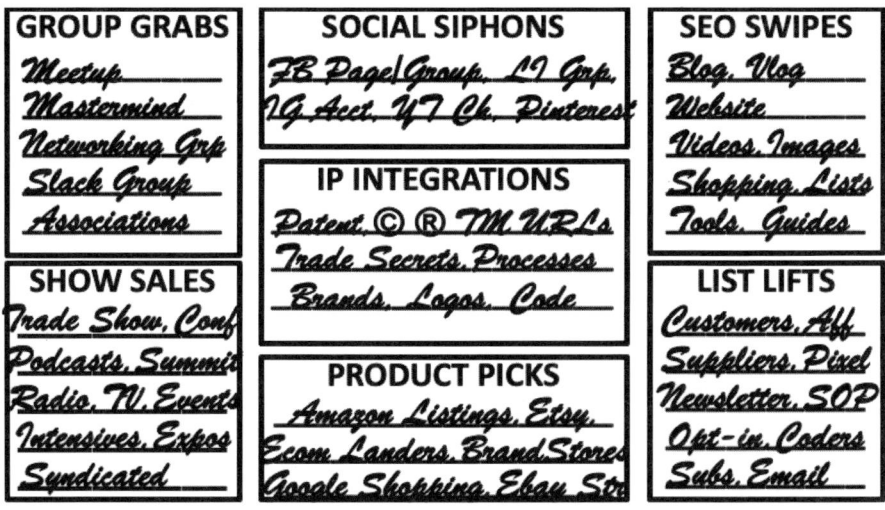

Fill out the $0 Traffic Assets Worksheet to figure out what traffic assets are available for you to buy.

GROUP GRABS	SOCIAL SIPHONS	SEO SWIPES
_____	_____	_____
_____	_____	_____
_____		_____
_____	**IP INTEGRATIONS**	_____
	_____	_____
SHOW SALES	_____	**LIST LIFTS**
_____	_____	_____
_____	**PRODUCT PICKS**	_____
_____	_____	_____
_____	_____	_____

Once you know what traffic assets you want to buy and you've completed the deal, follow these instructions for each platform to get administrative control.

HOW TO BUY A FACEBOOK PAGE:

Tools: Asset Purchase Agreement + Escrow.com
Seller Actions:

1. Have the Buyer like the page
2. From newsfeed choose "Your Pages" on top right
3. Click "Page Settings" from the top right menu bar
4. Choose "Page Roles" from the list on the left side of the page
5. Enter the Buyer's name in the "Assign a New Page Role" box
6. Click the "Editor" drop down next to their name
7. Select "Admin" to make them an admin
8. Click the "Add" button"
9. When you leave as admin they now own the page

HOW TO BUY A FACEBOOK AD ACCOUNT:

Tools: Asset Purchase Agreement + Escrow.com
Seller Actions:

1. Go to "Business Manager" settings in Facebook Business Manager
2. Click on "Ad Accounts"
3. Add the Buyer to the account as an Admin
4. Remove all the other existing Admins
5. Buyer now claims account from their Business Manager Account
6. Buyer enters Ad Account ID
7. Seller accepts ownership transfer request from notification they receive to accept the transfer request

HOW TO BUY AN INSTAGRAM ACCOUNT:

Tools: Asset Purchase Agreement + Escrow.com

Here are complete instructions: https://viralaccounts.com/transferring-ownership-of-instagram-accounts/

Note that it is safest to transfer the original email that established the account in addition to the Instagram account if you want to be sure that you have complete ownership.

HOW TO BUY A LINKEDIN GROUP:

Tools: Asset Purchase Agreement + Escrow.com
Seller Actions:

1. From the group homepage, select Manage group
2. Click "Admins" to see group owners + managers
3. Add Buyer as a Manager

4. Click "More" to the right of Buyer manager's name
5. Click "Transfer Ownership"
6. Click "Confirm" in the pop-up confirmation box

HOW TO BUY A MEETUP GROUP:

Tools: Asset Purchase Agreement + Escrow.com
Seller Actions:
1. From the Meetup group homepage, select Manage group
2. Choose Step Down as Organizer
3. In the search box, find the buyer name (must be a group member) and check the box beside their name, then hit Next
4. Click Select "Ask Selected Members"

Buyer Actions:
1. On Meetup group home page click "About"
2. Scroll down to "Organizer"
3. Click "Accept Nomination"

HOW TO BUY AN AMAZON PRODUCT:

Tools: Asset Purchase Agreement + Escrow.com
Seller Actions:
4. Change information in their account to that of the individual buying the account
5. Charge method (CC)
6. Deposit method (Bank Account)
7. Tax Information
8. Account Name
9. Email Address Associated

By doing the above, all customer ratings and reviews will be transferred and this includes services such as FBA.

You can do this all through Google for free, but here are a few other research tools (paid):

- DealStats Value Index
- BizComps
- BizMiner

BEFORE YOU MOVE ON TO THE NEXT SECTION:

1. **Google Category M&A:** Find what comparable companies like yours are buying.
2. **Get Crunchbase Trial:** Research what comparable companies are acquiring and investing in.
3. **Complete the Related Business Worksheet:** Find related business in 7 categories.
4. **Complete the $0 Traffic Assets Worksheet:** Find related media in 7 categories to acquire.

CHAPTER 3

HOW TO SOURCE DEALS

So far we've covered how to be an epic investor and how to find what businesses to buy. Now, we're going to go through two practice rounds of determining if a business is being sold for a bad, good, better, or great offer.

Here's where we are in the Deal Lifecycle:

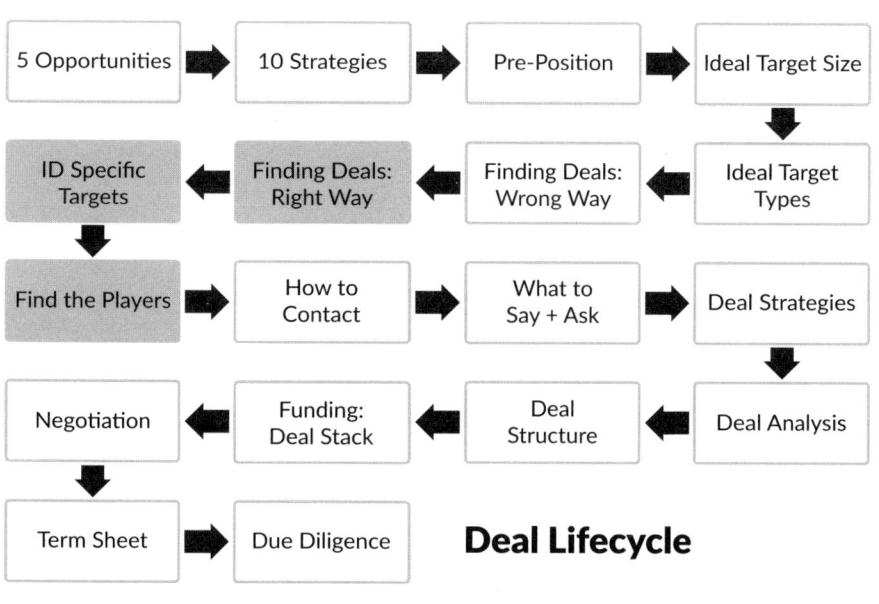

For these practice rounds, we're going to use business listing sites, BUT this is rarely how I find businesses to buy. These listing sites are better used as practice for figuring out what's a good deal or a bad deal, rather than purchasing a business. I'll show you in the next section how to cold outreach to businesses on your Related Businesses Worksheet and $0 Traffic Assets Worksheet.

DEAL SOURCING PRACTICE ROUND #1

Using BizBuySell.com, we'll search for established businesses for sale in the location we want (in this example, the location is San Diego). One of the search results is a pest control company. You'll see the listing information below. We're going to go through what's good, (outlined with a solid line), okay (outlined with a dashed line), and bad (outlined with a dotted box) about this listing.

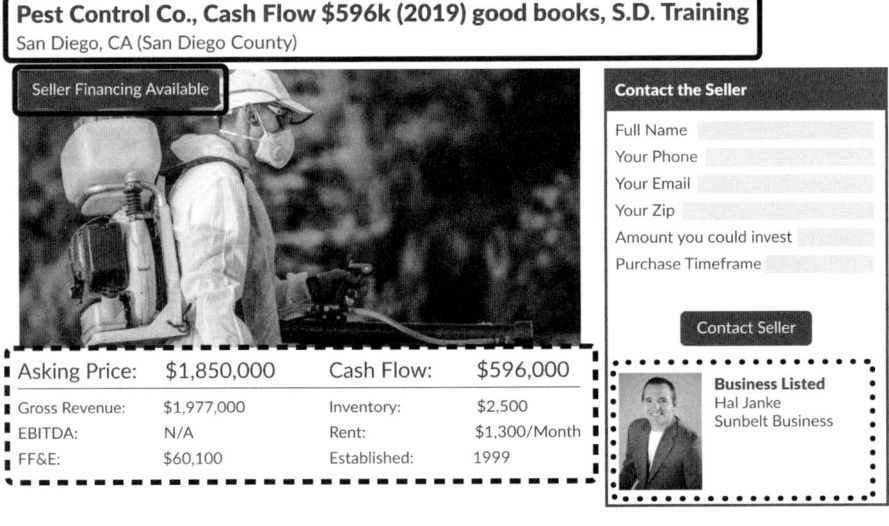

Pest Control Co., Cash Flow $596k (2019) good books, S.D. Training
San Diego, CA (San Diego County)

Seller Financing Available

Contact the Seller

Full Name
Your Phone
Your Email
Your Zip
Amount you could invest
Purchase Timeframe

Contact Seller

Asking Price:	$1,850,000	Cash Flow:	$596,000
Gross Revenue:	$1,977,000	Inventory:	$2,500
EBITDA:	N/A	Rent:	$1,300/Month
FF&E:	$60,100	Established:	1999

Business Listed
Hal Janke
Sunbelt Business

RF

Good (⸺):

1. The location matches where I'm looking to buy the business (San Diego)
2. Good books is a great sign because not every business has books—some still use paper and this makes figuring out financials difficult
3. Seller financing is great because we want to spend $0 out of pocket
4. It's a 3.1x multiple, which is in the range of businesses I like to buy (asking price divided by cashflow)
5. They have a 21-year history which means they're an established company
6. Rent is only $1,300/month which is pretty cheap and lowers overhead
7. FF&E (furniture, fixtures, and equipment) and inventory is included

Okay (– – –):

1. There's no EBITDA, which is usually a sign that this is an owner operated business, which is great for buying but bad if without the owner the business is difficult to manage

Bad (• • •):

1. I generally avoid all companies that have a broker, as the broker is trying to sell the company for as much as possible which isn't the environment you're trying to buy the business in

Business Description

Pest Control Co. Strong Net Cash Flow $596k, No exper. is req'd, S.D.

High Net Cash Flow of $596,000 (2019) A fast growing Pest Control company in San Diego, well established. Highly recognized with a very good following. Sales for 2019 are up from 2018 and the business continues to grow. Priced below market, this business has a great return on investment. (This Business is SBA pre-approved by Broker of Sunbelt.)

The Cashflow for 2019 will be closer to $596k if extrapolated through Dec. Cash flow in 2018 was $506k with a good strong steady growth in this business. With a new operator, fresh ideas and additional marketing there is even room to increase sales and earning. The business/owner has most all active accounts in the San Diego area. Broker has an SBA lender in place and prefers to use the Brokers lender. No Experience is Required owner will train.

Buyer requirements $1.2M Net Worth, $400k liquidity and a good credit score. Seller will carry a note of $200k at 6% interest for a determined period of time. The owner will stay on in a part-time capacity until the purchaser obtains their license.

Good (——) :

1. Cash flow is big plus
2. We know exactly what the terms of the note are upfront (although when they say a determined period of time instead of telling us the exact amount of time, it starts to become a red flag)

Bad (• • •) :

1. Sales for 2019 being up from 2018 is a red flag because financial statements can be (and frequently are) manipulated—we'd need to know that what they're actually up by

2. The broker who is selling this pre-approved the business, which doesn't mean anything and makes me question the broker

3. If I need to be trained to run the business, then I'm going to be working for a business—not above it

4. They're most likely going to ask for about 20% down on their asking price of $1,850,000, which is $400,000 upfront, and are going to be looking for a personal guarantee because of the request for a credit score

5. The owner has to train someone which means that there's nobody there right now that can do this when the owner leaves, which tells me that I'll have to find someone to run this company and that could be a challenge

6. If the owner leaves and we don't have our license yet we're at risk

Detailed Information

Location:	San Diego, CA
Inventory:	Included in asking price
Real Estate:	Leased
Building SF:	600
Lease Expiration:	N/A
Employees:	10
Furniture, Fixtures, & Equipment (FF&E):	Included in asking price
Facilities:	The business has a small office and a yard also.
Competition:	There are few competitors in the marketplace
Growth & Expansion:	Yes room to grow and expand with an aggressive owner
Financing:	200,000
Support & Training:	The owner will train for four weeks and then part-time up to six months with the new buyer.
Reason for Selling:	Personal

RF

Good (————) :

1. We like that the inventory is included
2. I like that the business has employees because I need somebody to come in and take the place of the owner (although because the owner says they need to train me and someone else isn't already trained isn't a great sign)

Okay (– – –) :

1. The office is leased
2. Few competitors is always a bonus—but can we trust this listing to be telling us that there aren't any other competitors for this company?

Bad (• • •) :

1. The office is really small so there's no room for expansion
2. If the owner is gone in 4 weeks after being around for 21 years, I'm going to have trouble building the relationships they initially had with their customers which could mean that I'm losing customers or unable to grow through referrals the way the original owner was able to

With all of that information, we can start to put together our analysis of this listing. We'll look at purchase price, seller finance, SBA 7a loan payment, down payment, cash flow, how much a manager will cost per year (using Glassdoor.com), and more to figure out if this business is worth buying.

Analysis Listing #1

Purchase Price	$1,850,000	**ROI**	
Seller Finance	($200,000)	**106.5%**	
SBA 7(a) @75%	($1,387,500)		
Down Payment	$262, 500	**Install $84k**	
Cash Flow	$596,000	**Manager**	
10% Int. 7-Yr. 100%*	($316,253)*		
Free Cash	**$279,747**	**ROI**	
Monthly Free Cash	**$ 23,313**	**74.6%**	

Combined payments on SBA 7A loan of $1,387,500 10% 7Yr = $23,034/month x 12 = $276,409.68 per year plus seller financing of $200k 10% 7Yr = $3,320.24/month x 12 = $39,842.88 per year

© 2020 Roland Frasier

This analysis shows that buying this pest control business isn't a terrible deal, although ideally we could get the seller to reduce the $262,500 down payment.

DEAL SOURCING PRACTICE ROUND #2

For this round, we're going to be looking at a Full-Service Fire Sprinkler System Contractor business that's for sale. Before we go any further, I'll say that right away I most likely wouldn't buy this business just because of the liability of the product. A business like this is going to require serious insurance and I tend to stay away from businesses that are this high risk when it comes to liability. But, for the practice round, let's go through and see what's good, okay, and bad about this deal.

Full-Service Fire Sprinkler System Contractor

San Diego, CA (San Diego County)

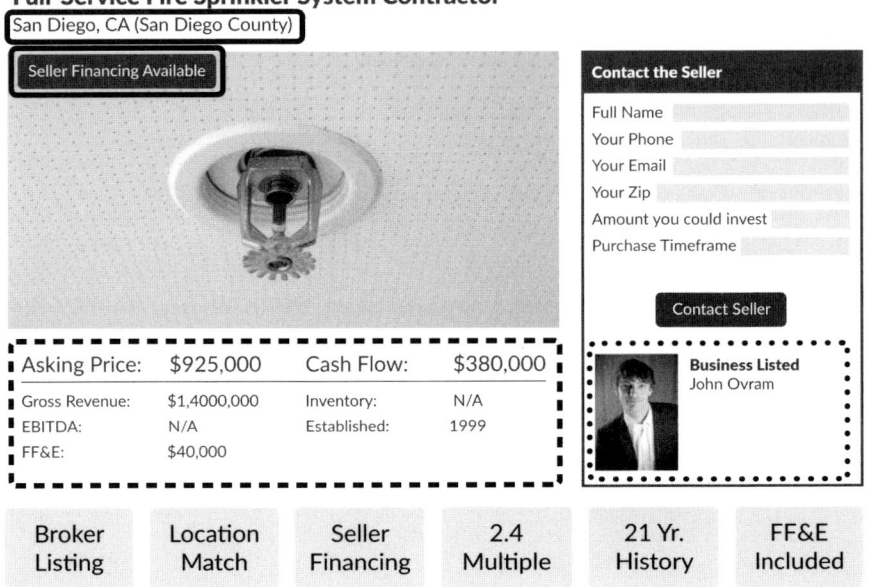

Seller Financing Available

Contact the Seller

Full Name
Your Phone
Your Email
Your Zip
Amount you could invest
Purchase Timeframe

Contact Seller

Asking Price:	$925,000	Cash Flow:	$380,000
Gross Revenue:	$1,4000,000	Inventory:	N/A
EBITDA:	N/A	Established:	1999
FF&E:	$40,000		

Business Listed
John Ovram

Broker Listing	Location Match	Seller Financing	2.4 Multiple	21 Yr. History	FF&E Included

Good (——) :

1. It's a location match (San Diego)
2. They're okay with seller financing
3. They're adding the FF&E
4. No EBITDA, so it's probably an owner operated business
5. 21-year history which means they're well established
6. 2.4x multiple which is in my ideal multiple range

Bad (• • •) :

1. They have a broker
2. They don't have any inventory
3. (Again) The business itself is a huge liability because of the service they offer, so there's going to be a huge insurance policy

RF

Business Description

Established over 10 years with great reputation for service and integrity. Company designs, installations, and offers fire sprinkler inspection/testing services. Average revenue mix is 56%. New Construction / 41% Tenant Improvements / 3% service. Services greater San Diego County up to San Bernardino and Riverside Counties.

Constituent annual revenue over $1M for last 4 years. Active owner is supported by team of eight full-time, non-union employees.

Financials:
2019: Sales = $1.4M (est); SDE = $380k (est)
2018: Sales = $1.2M; SDE = $247k
2017: Sales = $1.48M; SDE = $357k
2016: Sales = $1.4M ; SDE = $444k

Assets: Price includes approximately $40k in FF&E

Owner is retiring and will offer training period.

Good (——) :

1. I like that the business was established either twenty-one or ten years ago, but I don't like the inconsistency in the dates
2. We want the price to include FF&E

Okay (– – –) :

1. Consistent annual revenue over $1M is great, but we'd need to double check to make sure that this is true
2. Since the owner is retiring, we want to know where clients are currently coming from—if they're coming from his network then we're not going to have that inflow once he steps out from the company

Bad (• • •):

1. Fifty-six percent new construction means that if we go into a downcycle my business will drop by fifty percent (or more)
2. Forty-one percent tenant improvements also means that in a downcycle my business will also drop as tenants don't tend to move as often during these times
3. Only having 3% of contracts come from services tells me that we have minimal monthly contracts and recurring revenue
4. I personally like companies to have a minimum of 10 employees
5. In 2019 sales are in the same place as they were in 2016, telling me there hasn't been any growth in three years

Detailed Information

Location:	San Diego, CA
Employees:	8
Furniture, Fixtures, & Equipment (FF&E):	Included in asking price
Facilities:	Non-union shop operating out of 1,080 square foot facility, which includes admin office and warehouse space. Seller owns building and will offer fair market lease of $1,500/month to buyer.
Competition:	Current business philosophy has been to remain manageably small, due to owner's age and planning for retirement. Company does no marketing, and all customer acquisition is done through word-of-mouth referrals. A strategic marketing plan along with a salesperson are significant growth opportunities.
Support & Training:	Seller is retiring and will offer training
Reason for Selling:	Retirement
Business Website:	http://exitconsultinggroup.com/listing/fire-sprinkler-contractor/

Good (——) :

1. The seller owns the building, which is great because real estate is easy to finance

Bad (• • •) :

1. They want us to lease the building from them which means that we'll have to rent from the previous owner of the business, which isn't ideal
2. All customer acquisition is done through word-of-mouth which is a bad sign that they haven't been able to successfully market themselves and tells us they don't have predictable selling systems

Let's look at an analysis of this listing.

Analysis Listing #2

Purchase Price	$925,000	**ROI**	*Combined payments on SBA 7A loan of $693,750 10% 7Yr = $11,517/month x 12 = $138,204 per year plus seller financing of $138,750 10% 7Yr = $2,303.41/month x 12 = $27,640.92 per year*
Seller Finance	($138,750)	**231.5%%**	
SBA 7(a) @75%	($693,750)		
Down Payment	$92,500	**Install $84k Manager**	
Cash Flow	$380,000		
10% Int. 7-Yr. 100%*	($165,845)		
Free Cash	**$214,155**	**ROI**	
Monthly Free Cash	**$ 17,847**	**140.7%**	

Whoever buys this business shouldn't be looking for a platform, they should be looking for an add on to their contracting business or a means to buying a client list.

FINDING BUSINESSES AND KEY PLAYERS

Once you know what the green flags and red flags are when you buy a business, you can start to look at actual businesses that you'd be interested in buying. You might think that you need a huge network of business associates to be able to find these businesses—but you don't.

For each business that you're targeting (in every category of your Related Businesses Worksheet and $0 Traffic Assets Worksheet), there are 27 places to find your deals:

1. Friends
2. Family
3. Phone contacts
4. Instagram friends
5. LinkedIn contacts
6. Facebook friends
7. Email signature
8. Vistage
9. LinkedIn search/SN
10. Competitors
11. Distributors
12. People you meet
13. Networking groups
14. Messenger contacts
15. Angel networks
16. Financial planners
17. Direct mail
18. Trade associations
19. Customers
20. Suppliers
21. Masterminds
22. Contractors
23. Employees
24. EO
25. YPO
26. Hoovers
27. Trade events

As you narrow down the businesses that you're going to be looking to acquire, you'll start to create a list of the players that you need to contact in each business. To find the person to contact, go to the Terms of Service or Privacy Policy at the bottom of the business's website so that you can find out the actual name of the business.

Then, use these different strategies to find out who the key players for you to talk to are:

1. Call the company and ask who the owners are
2. Check the "About Us", "Team", or "Contact" page on their website
3. Google, "business permits" [city], [state]
4. Google, "certificate of occupancy" [city], [state]
5. Check Zoominfo.com
6. Search for the company on LinkedIn
7. Check SecStates.com for state business information
8. Google, "business licenses" [city], [state]
9. Check Hoovers
10. Google, "license inspections" [city], [state]
11. Source Using LinkedIn Sales Navigator to search specific details of each company

Use the Identify The Players Worksheet below:

Identify The Player(s)

Call the company and ask who the owners are.	Google "certificate of occupancy" [city], [state]	Google "business licenses" [city], [state]
Check "about us" "team" + "contact" on their website.	Check ZoomInfo.com	Check Hoovers
	Search the company on LinkedIn	Google "licenses inspections" [city], [state]
Google "business permits" [city], [state]	Check SecStates.com for state business information	

© 2020 Roland Frasier

BEFORE YOU MOVE ON
TO THE NEXT SECTION:

1. **Search BizBuySell.com:** Look at several businesses in your area by category.
2. **Analyze Each for Good and Bad:** Get familiar with the terms and what to look for in listings.
3. **Identify The Players Worksheet:** Complete this for each target principle you have identified.

CHAPTER 4

WHAT TO SAY TO KEY PLAYERS

Now it's time to start talking to business owners. If you're starting to feel a little nervous, that's okay—but you have to be willing to have these conversations to be an investor. If you're not ready to cold contact businesses you'll need to get a partner. This is an essential part of closing investment deals.

To make this process easier, I've included copy and paste templates that you can use when you reach out to prospects. The key to using these templates is to remember they need to be adapted to your voice. For example, if you're calling someone using one of the phone scripts below, read that phone script out loud before you call them. Make sure it sounds natural to your voice and change anything that makes it sound like you're reading from a script instead of genuinely speaking to the person on the other end of the call.

We've officially entered the What To Say + Ask part of the Deal Lifecycle.

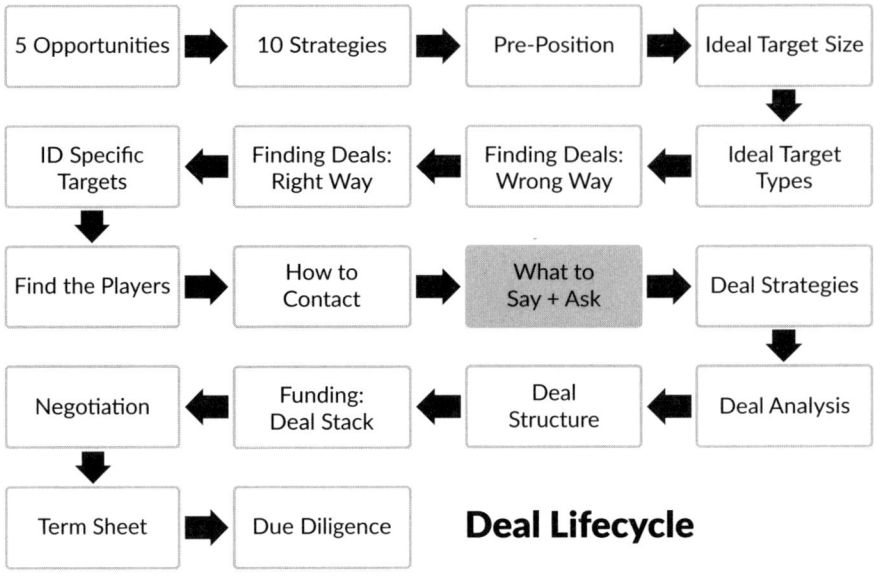

Deal Lifecycle

You're going to make initial contact with the company through one of these methods:

Get a warm introduction: Query your network and have someone who knows the person you want to contact connect you via phone, email, text

Make a phone call: Call the person you want to contact and follow the phone script below

Write a letter: Write a letter to the person you want to contact using the letter template below, then meet, call or Zoom

LinkedIn: Find them on LinkedIn, make a connection request or InMail, then try to move the conversation to meet, call or Zoom

Reach out on social: Find and message them on social media, then move to live chat, call, Zoom, etc.

When it comes to outreach, it's a numbers game. Don't be disheartened if people aren't interested or calling you back—for every 100 outreaches you'll close about 1-3 deals. As you become a more well known investor and your network grows, people will start to come to you with deals and you'll be able to increase the number that you can close. For example, I'm able to close about fifty-percent of my deals. Years of investing will snowball into a much higher percentage of deals.

It's A Numbers Game

100 Outreaches

60 Responses

10 Conversations

5 Offers

1-3 Deals

Below are the template and scripts that you'll use to contact cold leads.

Remember, these are just guidelines. It's your job to adapt them to you and make them sound natural to your voice. Practice reading them out loud and making the necessary tweaks that will make you sound authentic and confident.

LINKEDIN SCRIPTS

#1: LinkedIn Connect Request Option 1

"Hi [Their Name],

I'm an investor looking to invest in a [Industry] company, located in [Geography] with $X to $Y in top line revenue.

Your company name came up in my research and since you are a [Title] there, I'm requesting a connection to see if you might like to chat about the possibility of working together in some way.

If so, please connect and let me know a good time to chat."

#2: LinkedIn Connect Request Option 2

"Hi [Their Name],

I own a [industry] business and am looking for a [their business niche] business to refer my [customers/clients] to.

Your company came up in my research, and since you are a [Title] there, I'm requesting a connection to see if we can set up a time to chat to see if there is a fit.

Please connect and let me know a good time to chat."

Why This Works:

- Starting off by saying you're an investor shows you're not trying

to sell them something
- You show them that you know what their company does by talking about the industry
- You show you know where their business is actually located
- You tell them that you put effort into choosing the companies you are going to reach out by saying you researched them
- You have a call to action to connect
- You're showing them what you would want to chat about by initially telling them you're an investor

PHONE SCRIPTS

#1: Use this phone script for a cold call, not related to your current business:

"Hi my name is [Your name].

I'm a private investor looking to invest in a [type of company], located in [location] [Option #1] 'with between [$X] and [$Y] in top line revenue' or [Option 2] 'with profits between [$X] and [$Y]'. I'm looking to complete a transaction within the next 3-6 months.

Your company came up in my research, so I'm touching base to see if you might like to meet and chat about that."

#2: Use this phone script for a cold call, related to your current business:

"Hi, my name is [Your name].

I own a [Business Type] company in [Location] called [Company Name], and from time to time I have customers who are looking for [Target Business Product/Services].

I'd love to schedule a time to grab lunch next week to learn more about [Target Business] and see if we might do some business together. What does your schedule look like for next [Day], [Date], at X o'clock."

Or,

"Hi, my name is [Your name].

I'm a private investor looking to invest in a [Type of company] located in [location] [Option #1] 'with between [$X] and [$Y] in top line revenue' [or Option #2] 'with profits between [$X] and [$Y]'. I'm looking to complete a transaction within the next 3-6 months.

Your company came up in my research, so I'm touching base to see if you might like to meet. What does your schedule look like for next [Day], [Date], at X o'clock."

#3: Use this phone script for a cold call to a distressed business:

"HI, my name is [Your name].

I work with a group of wealthy investors who provide capital to companies.

We typically invest in, merge or acquire the companies we work with.

If this sounds like something that might interest you, I would love to set a time to discuss it in more detail."

Remember: Don't say that you're looking to invest in distressed companies. You'll make them feel embarrassed and like you're being predatory for their company, instead of trying to help them.

WANT TO GRAB A COPY OF THE SCRIPT TEMPLATES?

HEAD ON OVER TO ETHICALLYPROFIT.COM/BOOK AND GRAB THEM NOW!

LETTER TEMPLATES

When sending a letter as an investor, you want to avoid sending the letter to their business address. If their business is listed for sale, their employees might not be aware and you'll create a huge problem for them. You don't want to be a problem, you want to be a solution.

Another bonus of sending a letter to their home instead of business is that you'll be able to get past any gatekeepers and keep the conversation between yourselves in case they're having challenges with partners.

It's important that your letter tells them why you're writing to them at their home address, instead of their business address. This builds trust and respect. If there are more than one key player or director listed for the company, send a letter to all of their home addresses.

#1: Use this letter template for a cold contact, not related to your current business:

"Dear [Their name],

I'm a private investor looking to invest or acquire a [type of company], in [location] [Option #1] 'with between [$X] and [$Y] in top line revenue' [or Option #2] 'with profits between [$X] and [$Y]'. I'm looking to complete a transaction within the next 3-6 months.

Your company came up in my research as a possible investment opportunity, and I'm writing to see if you might be interested in receiving an investment in [Company Name]. I'm writing to you at this address, which I found in the company public records, to maintain confidentiality of our discussions from your employees.

If this is of interest, please let me know and we can set up a time for a call to explore the possibilities. You can call me at (##) ###-#### at your convenience, and I will touch base on [Day], [Date], if I don't hear back from you before then.

Sincerely,
Your Name"

#2: Use this letter template for a cold contact, related to your current business:

"Dear [Their Name],

I own a [Business Type] company in [Location] called [Company Name], and from time to time I have customers who are looking for [Target Business Products/Services].

I'd love to schedule a time to [chat on the phone/grab lunch] next week to learn more about [Target Business] and see if we might do some business together. What does your schedule look like for next [Day], [Date] at X o'clock?

Sincerely,
[Your Name]"

#3: Use this letter template for a cold contact to a distressed business:

"Dear [Their Name],

I'm a private investor, looking to invest or acquire a company like yours that might be able to use a capital infusion. Many great businesses have challenges getting traditional bank financing and I provide a faster, easier alternative to that.

Your company came up in my research as a possible investment opportunity, and I'm writing to see if you might be interested in receiving an investment or even selling [Company Name]. I'm writing to you at this address, which I found in the company public records, to maintain confidentiality of our discussions from your employees.

If interested, please let me know and let's set a time to chat on the phone to explore the possibilities. You can call me at (###) ###-#### at your convenience, and I will touch base on [DAY], [DATE] if I don't hear back from you before then.

Sincerely,
[Your Name]"

RF

BEFORE YOU MOVE ON
TO THE NEXT SECTION:

(Overachievers 5x the numbers below)

1. **Send 1 LinkedIn Connect Request to Whoever You Have Identified**
2. **Send 1 LinkedIn InMail** (if you have InMails)
3. **Send 1 Message to a Zero Dollar Traffic Asset**
4. **Make 1 Phone Call**
5. **Send 1 Letter**

CHAPTER 5
ANALYSIS AND FUNDING

This is the last section of this book, making you one step away from learning everything you need to know to be an epic investor. So far we've covered how to turn a crisis into opportunity, where to find businesses to buy (both related and traffic assets), and what you'll say to the key decision makers of a business you're interested in acquiring.

This puts us at the Deal Analysis and Deal Stack (Funding) steps of the Deal Lifecycle.

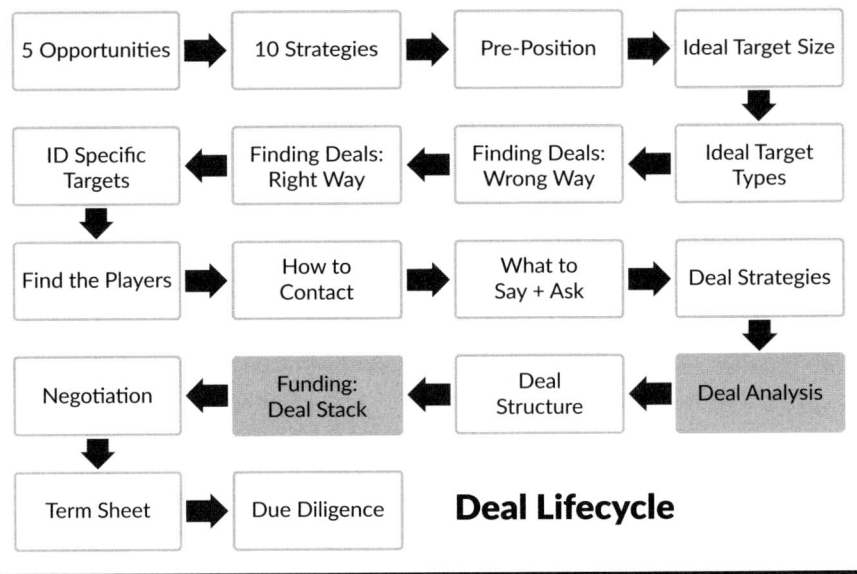

Deal Lifecycle

First, we'll cover how to make an analysis to let you know what funding you'll need. Then, I'll show you how to pay $0 out of pocket by deal stacking.

MAKING AN ANALYSIS

Your analysis is going to start with the multiple (asking price divided by the cash flow). This multiple will tell you if the business is in your multiple range or not. I primarily buy businesses with a maximum 3.7x multiple.

Here's an idea of what different industries are selling at based on multiples. You can use this in your Related Businesses Worksheet to see what multiples to expect to buy businesses in for different industries (media, IP, product vendors, etc.).

Revenue Multiples By Industry

Industry Name	EV/Sales	Industry Name	EV/Sales
Advertising	1.83	Chemical (Basic)	1.52
Aerospace/Defense	2.01	Chemical (Diversified)	1.72
Air Transport	1.97	Chemical (Specialty)	3.27
Apparel	2.03	Coal & Related Energy	1.08
Auto & Truck	3.58	Computer Services	1.43
Auto Parts	1.60	Entertainment	6.81
Bank (Money Center)	5.32	Environmental & Waste Services	3.34
Banks (Regional)	4.47	Farming/Agriculture	1.35
Beverage (Alcoholic)	5.30	Financial Svcs. (Non-bank &Insu	31.49
Beverage (Soft)	5.08	Food Processing	2.19
Broadcasting	2.08	Food Wholesalers	0.54
Brokerage & Investment Banking	4.93	Furn/Home Furnishings	1.31
Building Materials	2.00	Green & Renewable Energy	13.15
Business & Consumer Services	2.97	Healthcare Products	7.42
Cable TV	3.85	Healthcare Support Services	0.68

See full list here: http://pages.stern.nyu.edu/~adamodar/New_Home_Page/datafile/psdata.html

When making your analysis, you're also going to look at the EBITDA of the seller's business. You can use the chart below to find the EBITDA multiple based on industry. If you don't see your industry here, you can call the trade association and find out if they have EBITDA averages. This is going to give you a guide for the profit of the company you're looking at.

RF

EBITDA Multiples By Industry

Industry Name	EV/Sales	Industry Name	EV/Sales
Advertising	8.86	Coal & Related Energy	5.79
Aerospace/Defense	12.15	Computer Services	10.70
Air Transport	34.43	Computers/Peripherals	24.76
Apparel	14.69	Construction Supplies	15.23
Auto & Truck	45.73	Diversified	11.37
Auto Parts	10.07	Drugs (Biotechnology)	14.40
Beverage (Alcoholic)	17.61	Drugs (Pharmaceutical)	14.32
Beverage (Soft)	20.74	Education	14.43
Broadcasting	7.84	Electrical Equipment	15.96
Building Materials	13.27	Electronics (Consumer & Office)	18.96
Business & Consumer Services	17.40	Electronics (General)	17.52
Cable TV	11.11	Engineering/Construction	10.85
Chemical (Basic)	10.01	Entertainment	36.26
Chemical (Diversified)	13.38	Environmental & Waste Services	14.98
Chemical (Specialty)	15.56	Farming/Agriculture	14.71

See full list here: http://pages.stern.nyu.edu/~adamodar/New_Home_Page/datafile/vebitda.html

Knowing the industry multiple and EBITDA multiple, you can ask yourself if this is a reasonable deal and a worthy investment of your time in trying to land it. To answer that question, fill in all of the blanks below.

Is _____ x SDE/EBITDA Price Reasonable?

Asking $ _____
Real Estate ($ _____)
Net Ask $ _____
/SDE-EBITDA $ _____
Ask multiple _____ Industry _____

Note: I subtract real estate from the asking price so I can see what the company is worth without the added real estate asset.

If this makes sense so far, the next step in your conversation with the seller will be to sign an NDA and receive their financial statements. You'll need their Balance Sheet (assets and liabilities and owners/shareholders equity), P&L income statement, and a statement of cash flows).

Once you have this information, fill in this Target Analysis Profile Sheet:

Your Target Analysis Profile

Cash	$	Ask	, SDE $	M=	
Acct. Receivable	$	$	Sales, $		ARR
Note Receivable	$	AP = $	, RE NP = $		
CD/MM/TB	$	Def. IP			
Securities	$	Runs	shifts @	% capacity	
Raw Materials	$	Mkt via			
Work in Progress	$	Sell via			
Inventory	$	CEO	COO	CFO	
FF&E	$		customers	prospects	
Vehicles	$	Seller RFL			
Real Estate	$	Wants			

On the left:

Cash: Amount of available money

Acct. Receivable: Short term, small amounts of money owed

Note Receivable: Longer, larger amounts of money owed

CD/MM/TB: Certificate of deposit, money market, treasury bills

Raw Materials: Cost of raw materials AND the market value
> Ex. A restaurant has $30,000 in raw fish, but if they don't sell it before it goes bad, the market value is $0

Work in Process: Anything that is in the middle of being built
> Ex. An IT company that provides IT services work in process is a 3-month contract that hasn't expired yet

Inventory: Included inventory

FF&E: Included FF&E
    Ex. Furniture, Fixtures, and Equipment

Vehicles: Owned vehicles

Real Estate: Own real estate

On the right:

SDE = EBITDA (Profit)

M = Multiple

Sales = Net sales

ARR = Annual Recurring Revenue

AP = Accounts Payable (on balance sheet)

RE NP = Real estate notes payable (on balance sheet)

Def. IP = Defensible IP that is patented technology, product, etc. (not on financial statements)

Runs = How often a machine is being used, for how many shifts and at what capacity is it running at (the goal is to find out how much in sales could you increase by before you have to buy additional machines, equipment, or labor)

Mkt via = How are they marketing?

Sell via = How are they selling?

CEO, COO, CFO = Are these individuals staying or going?

Customers = How many active customers?

Prospects = How many prospects are in their pipeline?

Seller RFL = What's the seller's reason for leaving?

Wants = What does the seller want to do with the money?

Note: The more you can get the seller to tell you what they want to do with the money or their time when they retire from the business, the happier they'll be to talk with you. They'll also tell you a lot of good information that will tell you how to frame your offer.

Once you've done your analysis and gotten to the point that your Target Analysis Profile is filled out, it's time to fund the deal so that you pay $0 out of pocket for this company.

FUNDING THE DEAL

At this point, I'm sure you're wondering what the magic is behind buying companies for $0 out of pocket. Here's the answer: deal stacking.

I have 159 different strategies to acquire businesses without paying out of pocket for them, and I'll stack these strategies on top of each other to achieve the $0 out of pocket. While it sounds hard to believe, this is something that is happening around you all of the time. All you need to be aware of are those strategies for deal stacking.

I call these strategies my Tool Stack and I'm going to share 15 of them with you below.

THE DEAL STACK: 15 WAYS TO ACQUIRE BUSINESSES FOR $0 OUT OF POCKET

Since we're doing deals through research and cold calling, the chances of there being another business trying to acquire the one you're targeting are slim. This gives you even more opportunity to deal stack, even asking the seller to defer down payments.

Here are the 15 ways you can acquire a business for $0 out of pocket, by using the tools in my Tool Stack.

#1: Carve Outs

Carve outs involve "carving out" the assets that you don't want included in the deal. For example, you can carve out working capital that you don't need, equipment, inventory, and more. This takes the price of these assets out of the asking prices and reduces the purchase price.

#2: Accounts Receivables Financing (AR Financing)

Based on what customers owe the company, you can carve out these Accounts Receivables and tell the seller that they can keep that money when it comes in, if they remove it from the purchase price. Just remember that this will reduce your incoming cash flow, so only do this if you know you don't need that money.

#3: Real Estate Sale/Leaseback

If a deal involves $1 million in real estate, you can carve out that real estate from the deal or sell the real estate after the deal. You can then lease back the real estate by cutting a deal with the new owner.

#4: Earn-In Equity

You can provide services to a business in exchange for equity. For example, I just did an earn-in deal as a consultant to help with a business, earning myself into a 25% share in that business.

#5: Owner Carry

You'll owe the seller of the business money (through seller financing), instead of owing it to the bank or lenders. The seller will have a 40-90% in a promissory note that you'll pay to them.

#6: Deferred Down Payments

Deferred down payments (DDP) are similar to seller financing, since the buyer will owe the seller money. The difference is that DDP are for shorter periods of time.

#7: Baseline

A baseline helps you acquire someone's business, but they'll still own part of it. You don't take away any profit that they currently have, but you'll do a 50/50 split on any profit in excess of current profits. Generally, this is when you hit 3x profit.

#8: Earnout

When a seller and a buyer can't agree on a price because the seller believes there will be an upcoming upward hockey stick curve in the near future (even though those profits aren't promised), you can use an earnout. The seller and the buyer will agree the buyer will pay the seller an earnout if the business performs as they believe and hits a certain level. Then, they'll get an additional payment down the road.

#9: Pipe Wrench

If you're constantly sending new business to another company, you ask them to give you part of their company in return for continuing to send business to them.

#10: Inventory Consignment

If the company has $100k of inventory, you can carve out that inventory and tell the seller that you'll pay for that inventory as it sells. You'll hold it for them and as it sells you'll pay the value of the cost of that inventory.

#11: Asset Based Lending

Asset based lending (ABL) finances equipment or other assets to fund the business.

#12: Supplier Loan

Supplier loans come from suppliers of products to that business. These are leveraged by asking the supplier for a loan in return for you continuing to use them to receive your supplies from them versus a competitor.

#13: Revenue Based Financing

This is funding based on revenue and is commonly done by credit card companies. They'll give you a loan and then you'll pay it back at an agreed upon rate.

#14: Integrator Equity

Integrator Equity is given to somebody that runs the company and in return for their work they'll get equity.

#15: Private Place Memorandum

A private placement memorandum (PPM) sells part of the company to another group of investors, so you can use that money to cover your funding.

These are 15 of the 159 ways that I acquire businesses with $0 out of pocket. Remember, you want to deal stack—use as many of these as you need to reach that $0 and stay creative. There are always ways to lower the asking price or to spend less money outfront, you just need to be asking yourself the right questions to get there.

Let's look at some case studies of businesses that I've acquired for $0 out of pocket. Below are 5 case studies where you'll see the asking price and how we got creative to spend $0 on each acquisition.

CASE STUDIES IN FUNDING

Case Study #1: $250,000 Ask for a 250k Member Facebook Group for $0 OOP

$250k Ask for 253,000 member Facebook Group

$1.5K offer with Deferred Down Payment

$1.5K paid in 30 days from Cash Flow

Case Study #2: $125,000 Ask for a 53,000 Member Facebook Group for $0 OOP

$125K Ask 53k Member FB Group

$75K Purchase Price Agreed

$70K RBF First Funds In From Cash Flow

$50K 1-Year Sponsorship to a mortgage broker

$20K 1-Year Sponsorship to a training company

$5k Split Equity and CC Cash Advance

Case Study #3: $5 million Mail House for $0 OOP

$5M 28-Year Old Mail House

10%+ Revenue from our referrals

20% Pipe Wrench = $1M Value

2% Earn-In per $1M Incremental Cash flow

Case Study #4: $300,000 SaaS for $0 OOP

$300K 3-Year Old SaaS vendor to one of our companies

$100k Purchase Price

$90k-10k month owner carry for 9 months

$10k DDP funded in 1 week from 1st email

Case Study #5: $3M Publisher with a $3.9M Ask for $0 OOP

$3M Publishing House ($1.3M EBITDA)

$2M Acquisition Price (1.5x EBITDA)
$1.6M 80% Owner Carry 3 year balloon at 0%
$400k 20% DDP (30 days)
$400k 3PL 3 year 10% interest only no warrants
$800K Integrator Equity Sale 20% (3x valuation)
Own 80% for $0 OOP + $360k cash

By analyzing deals and using deal stacks, you can make sure that you're getting a good deal and figure out creative ways to pay zero dollars out of pocket for your acquisitions. This makes it much easier to acquire more businesses on your Related Businesses Worksheet and $0 Traffic Assets, so that you're able to continue to work above your business, not for it or on it.

CONCLUSION
TO THE EPIC INVESTORS...

Being an epic investor requires a mindset away from working for your business or on your business. But, it also requires something else. You have to be willing to look at the world differently when everyone else is worried about spending their money.

While COVID-19 has started a recession in the USA, time and time again we've seen the same pattern post recession. The GDP comes right back up, and we're able to continue with our economy as we were before.

Except you were able to buy a business at its lowest valuation, and then reap the benefits as the economy brings that valuation higher than it was when you bought it. That's what being an epic investor is all about.

You're going to see the opportunity, and then create a way to acquire businesses with little risk to you—especially when you use an SPV and the $0 OOP Tool Stack.

You've officially learned everything you need to know to become an epic investor and turn crisis into opportunities for yourself, your family, and your business.

Now, it's time to start looking for some businesses to buy.

RF

READY FOR MORE?
JOIN THE EPIC CHALLENGE TODAY!

During this 5 day challenge, we will be focusing on how to Ethically Profit In Crisis.

And after 5 days you will leave with a list of at least 5 laser-focused acquisition opportunities to add to your portfolio.

I will walk you through every step of the way on LIVE coaching calls...

1. We will focus on where to even start...
2. How to find businesses that are open to deals (and one's that don't even know yet that they are)...
3. How to approach the right people...
4. And how to creatively put together a deal in which everyone wins.

And it's all done through a step-by-step road map tailored just for you.

So if you are ready to get focused, take action, and win – I want you to join me in our 5 day EPIC Challenge.

I am so excited to share this process with you...because I know the power and potential it has for you as well as the impact it can make on others around you.

Imagine what's possible when I take you through my 30 years of experience in just 5 days and leave you ready to make your first (or next) acquisition.

What would it mean to you to not only see this process...

But take powerful daily action over these 5 days with support from myself and hundreds of other entrepreneurs from all around the world?

Join the 5-Day EPIC Challenge Here: myepicchallenge.com

RF

WANT MORE ACTIONABLE TOOLS, STRATEGIES, AND CONTENT TO HELP YOU GROW AND SCALE YOUR COMPANY?

CHECK OUT THE LINKS BELOW...

Grab All The Resources Talked About In The Book Here:
ethicallyprofit.com/book

Scalable.co:
We Help "Accidental Entrepreneurs" Scale Their Companies From $1M to $10M...and Beyond.

RolandFrasier.com:
Actionable Tools & Strategies To Help You Profit From Change

BusinessLunchPodcast.com:
This Is Your Seat At The Table! Join Roland As He Shares Exclusive Content To Help Grow Your Business And Interviews Industry Leaders Like Sir Richard Branson, Sara Blakely, and Arnold Schwarzenegger.

Follow Roland On Social:
Youtube: www.youtube.com/RolandFrasiers/
LinkedIn: www.linkedin.com/in/rolandfrasier/
Twitter: @rolandfrasier
Facebook: www.facebook.com/RolandFrasierPage
Instagram: @rolandfrasier

GLOSSARY OF TERMS

3P: Third-party

4DCM: 4 Day Cash Machine

4DX: 4 Disciplines Of Execution (from Stephen R. Covey and Chris McChsney's book: "The 4 Disciplines of Execution")

ABL: Asset Based Lending

ADR: American Depositary Receipt

ADS: American Depositary Share

AGM: Annual General Meeting

AML: Anti-Money Laundering

AP: Accounts Payable

APA: Asset Purchase Agreement

AR: Accounts Receivable

ARR: Annual Recurring Revenue

BK: Bankruptcy

BNI: Business Network International

CA: Confidentiality Agreement

CAGR: Compound Annual Growth Rate

CB: Crunchbase (when reviewing EPIC presentation slides)

CBF: Customer-Based Funding

CC: Credit Card

CD: Certificate of Deposit (https://www.investopedia.com/terms/c/certificateofdeposit.asp)

CEO: Chief Executive Officer

CFC: Controlled Foreign Association

CFIUS: Committee on Foreign Investment in the United States

CFO: Chief Financial Officer

CGT: Capital Gains Tax

CIC: Change In Control

CIM: Confidential Information Memorandum

CIO: Chief Information Officer

CIP: Cash In Pocket

CMO: Chief Marketing Officer

CNC: Covenant Not To Compete

COC: Change Of Control

COGS: Cost Of Goods Sold

COO: Chief Operating Officer

CPC: Cost Per Click

CPM: Cost Per Mille (AKA Cost Per Thousand Impressions)

CRO: Conversion Rate Optimization

CTO: Cost To Own

CVJ: Customer Value Journey

CVR: Contingent Value Right

CX: Customer

CXO: Chief Experience Officer

DCF: Discounted Cashflow

DD: Due Diligence (if topic is about receiving money, this can also be "Direct Deposit")

DDP: Deferred Down Payment

DDT: Debt Double Tap

DGCL: Delware General Corporation Law

DLLCA: Delaware Limited Liability Act

DP: Down Payment

DTC: Depository Trust Company

E2P: Enterprise to Person

EB5: Employment-based fifth preference category (https://en.wikipedia.org/wiki/EB-5_visa#:~:text=The%20United%20States%20EB%2D5,by%20investing%20at%20least%20%24900%2C000)

EBIT: Earnings Before Interest & Tax

EBITDA: Earnings Before Interest, Taxes, Depreciation & Amortization

EBT: Earnings Before Tax

EDGAR: Electronic Data Gathering, Analysis and Retrieval

EI: Earn-In

EIDL: Economic Injury Disaster Loan

EO: Exempt Organizations

EOI: Expression Of Interest

EOIQ: Expression Of Interest Questionnaire

ESOP: Employee Stock Ownership Plan

EV: Enterprise Value

FB: Facebook

FF&E: Furniture, Fixtures & Equipment

RF

FMV: Fair Market Value

FYE: Fiscal Year End

HELOC: Home Equity Line Of Credit

ICP: Ideal Customer Profile

IG: Instagram

IM: Information Memorandum (could also be "Instant Message" depending on context)

IOI: Indication Of Interest

IP: Intellectual Property

IPO: Initial Public Offering

IRA: Individual Retirement Account

JIT: Just In Time

JV: Joint Venture

LB: Lease Back

LBO: Leveraged Buyout

LI: Linkedin

LLC: Limited Liability Corporation

LOC: Line Of Credit

LOI: Letter Of Intent

LTM: Last Twelve Months

M: Multiple

M&A: Mergers & Acquisitions

MBF: Merchant Based Financing

MBI: Management Buy-In

MBO: Management Buyout

MD&A: Management Discussion & Analysis

MIA: Market Impact Assessment

MOM: Month-Over-Month

MOOVS: Manager/ Owner Operator Value Swap

MRR: Monthly Recurring Revenue

NCA: Non-Compete Agreement

NCC: Non-Compete Clause

NDA: Non-Disclosure Agreement

NLP: Neuro Linguistic Programing (https://en.wikipedia.org/wiki/Neuro-linguistic_programming)

NP: Notes Payable

NPS: Net Promoter Score

NR: Notes Receivable

OC: Owner Carry

OKR: Objectives & Key Results

OM: Offering Memorandum

OOP: Out Of Pocket

OPM: Other Peoples Money

PE: Private Equity

PI: Post-Integration

PMN: Private Money Note

PO: Purchase Order

PPC: Pay Per Click

PPM: Private Placement Memorandum

PPP: Paycheck Protection Program

PSA: Purchase & Sale Agreement

PSS: Product Service System

Q1,2,3,4: Quarter 1, 2, 3 and/ or 4 (each quarter lasts 3 months for a total of 4 Quarters or 12 months)

R/R: Risk vs. Reward

RBF: Revenue Based Financing

RE: Real Estate

RE SLB: Real Estate Sale & Leaseback

REI: Real Estate Investment

ROAS: Return On Ad Spend

ROBS: Roll-Over As Business

ROI: Return On Investment

SAM: Serviceable Available Market

SBA: Small Business Administration (small business loan)

SCORE: Service Corps of Retired Executives

SDE: Seller's Discretionary Earnings

SLB: Sale & Lease Back (or Seller Lease Back depending on the context)

SLiP: Self Liquidating Loan

SME: Small & Mid-size Enterprises

SN: Search Navigator (in relation to Linkedin)

SOP: Standard Operating Procedure

SPA: Share Purchase Agreement

SPV: Special Purpose Vehicle

TAM: Total Available Market or Total Addressable Market

TB: Trial Balance

TBD: To Be Determined, To Be Declared, To Be Decided, To Be Denounced, To Be Disclosed, To Be Done (depends on context)

TEV: Total Enterprise Value

TOA: Terms Of Agreement

TOS: Terms Of Service

RF

VC: Venture Capital

VOC: Voice Of Customer

VTB: Vendor Take Back

VWAP: Volume Weighted Average Price

WHL: Warehouse & Logistics

WIP: Work-In-Progress

WWYDWTM: What Would You Do With The Money

YOY: Year-Over-Year

YPO: Young President's Organization

YT: Youtube